THE LYCH-GATE

Songs and Sonnets of Autumn

D J Etchell holds several qualifications in science and in classics from various universities. He has also published *Sonnets from the Iliad*, a translation of Homer's *Iliad* into 317 sonnets.

He lives in splendid seclusion with his wife Jean and dog Smudge in the North of England.

Also by D J Etchell

Sonnets from the Iliad

THE LYCH-GATE

Songs and Sonnets of Autumn

D J Etchell

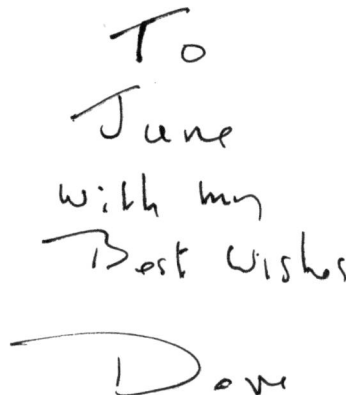

To
June
with my
Best wishes

Dave

Burghwallis Books

First published in 2009 by Burghwallis Books

Cover Illustration: The Lych-gate, St Helen's Church,
Burghwallis, by Brian Glidden

ISBN 978-0-9560838-2-1

Proofreading, design and dtp by
Mushroom Publishing, Bath, UK
mail@mushroompublishing.com

Printed and bound by
Lightning Source

For Jean

Contents

Foreword

"Oh Wild West Wind, thou breath of autumn's being..."
"Season of mists and mellow fruitfulness!"

So begin two of the greatest poems ever written in our language! These are the words of young men; of poets unafraid to use 'High English' in all its luxuriant glory. The poems are romantic and unselfconscious in style. Their rhythms flow like liquid silver with intoxicating beauty from line to line. Here, we decidedly do not have the limpness or obscurity which has characterised much of the poetry of the twentieth, and the present, centuries.

My poems consciously attempt to scale these sublime heights. An attempt doomed to fail, of course, as it stands next to and must be compared with the distilled essence of the genius of Keats, Shelley and the other greats of English poetry.

The poems are largely those of autumn and of the philosophical reflections which the season brings; with its fulfilment and death, beauty and decay. Some of them are highly personal in nature.

This season for me has always been a time of heightened sensitivity and awareness, when poetic instincts seem to go into overdrive as I am enveloped by the awareness of my mortality as the long shadows creep earlier and earlier through the dying days.

Much of the inspiration for the poems comes from the quiet splendour of the old village of Burghwallis. Most of them were produced during many of the beautiful late summers and autumns which I have been privileged to see here. The area is alive for me with memories of walks with our dogs down its lanes and wooded paths, and with many other gifted sights of nature's beauty.

DJE

Summer's Departure

A liquid silken greying of the days
Draws mist around sad summers afterglow;
That jocund rascal lingers in the haze
Above spiked stubble, where late poppies blow.
Now summoned sunwards from this cooling air
To southlands till the Earth can turn again:
Departing swallows usher in despair
As lonely shadows, empty eaves, reclaim.
Around me beauty; yet with aching heart
I drink the glory of the dying leaves
For dearth will rule as golden days depart
To leave behind such poignant memories.
     Of youth, of wine, of music oh so sweet;
     Of vanished summer, when I was complete.

Titania's farewell

Now sad Titania bids farewell
For magic dies when autumn comes, tonight.
Curling wisps of wraith-like mist will break her spell
And shroud her glades in silent sad samite.
For the air grows chill and the leaves grow pale
And my heart aches so as house martins go
On their long journey as the light begins to fail;
In these mournful days when the sun sinks ever low.
Wilting blooms now crown her brow and heavy fruits,
Purple and black, droop from a gown grown old;
For the earth must rest till spring's waking shoots
Form a garland green where now hangs one of gold.
    Soon she must dream through all winter long,
    Till the vernal kiss of lord Oberon.

Yes, autumn comes

Hawthorne leaves with scarlet flame
Burn in the languid realm of rain;
Which seems with clouds of gentle grey
To close the door through which has stepped
Reluctant summer's final golden day.
Yes, autumn comes.

The twilight floods my wooded halls,
Half shadows fall on moss stained walls;
Ill with the dream of death's despair
For equinox again has passed
And life's pale legend wanders, who knows where?
For autumn comes.

Now with raven spreading wings
Night will descend, its coming brings
Thoughts of brief mortality:
That fate which waits when time must end
And love's fond memoried eyes no longer see.
Our autumn comes!

Dangerous Yellow

Now the leaves on the birch are a dangerous yellow,
Telling that autumn is here.
Though the trees are still full the days are grown mellow —
There's an ache in the heart of the year.

The holly seems dark and the old ivy sullen
Alone in their wintering green.
The willows are weary and dry verges coarsen,
All mourn for a beauty that's been.

For the splendour of summer, like that of a woman,
Is sensual joy at full prime.
But autumn's soft beauty brings pain with its omen
Of loss now as all things decline.

Unfinished Sonnet
Written 4.17-4.41 am, Sept 2007

With stark pale silent beauty moonlight floods
Across the limestone flags, beneath the trees.
The air is still, no leaves stir in the woods
As small hours cloak a world at restful ease.

My mind plays tricks; I see the holly — green
And through its barbs, where church lords o'er the dead
The ghosts of summer's hopes, forlorn, are seen;
Imagined, when those spirit beams have fled.

I drink this gift: a world in quietude;
With all at rest: a world in still repose.
And I awake, alone, in midnight mood,
Drift where my black thoughts restless current flows.

Harvest Gathered

The stubble runs in flaxen rows
Down fields where lazy sunlight glows —
And restless time, now languid, flows.

Soon slews the plough and gold gives way
To coruscations of the clay —
From ochre red to corpse-like grey.

Last days of summer gently fade
As swallows group with farewells made —
To barren field and ripened glade.

The moon stands mellow, nights are warm,
Soon comes the dying — waits the worm —
Till from this despond spring is born.

Autumn Song

September now, a yellow leaf hangs bright
Upon a dying beech. The first of many
Soon to fall and gladden autumn with the sight:
Of woods and bridle-ways made bonny,
With dying colours tossed in windblown heaps.
There: 'hectic reds' of Shelley lie — upon
Those 'half reaped furrows' dreamed by Keats —
In his peerless, perfect, autumn song.
Beauty, sadness of decline, must claim each year
Both yours and mine; lost poets all become in time
Our words like leaves, forgotten, musty, sere;
Yet theirs remain forever fresh, sublime.
    They found that truth was beauty, beauty truth;
    Bequeathing verse immortal, born of youth.

The Gentle Month

Sabre clouds are racing,
Slicing, through the blue,
Sharpened on the whetstone of the wind.
Raucous-rooks swoop raggedly
And quarrelsomely cue,
My restless autumn to its fatal end.

Oh summer's restless seeking
For wild love: where are you?
That rage of wanton lips and wild perfume.
Lost ecstasies of youth's long vanished dreams
Foreshadowed what we knew—
A perfect rose must wither in time's gloom.

That gentle month: September,
Has melted like the dew
Seduced by autumn to a rich decline;
Forlornly leaves are scattered,
Withered, pale of hue,
Death's last dowry, rotting and malign!

Dark auguries of winter,
Walk with me as I rue
Those pathway's, chosen? Or predestined still.
The nights grow long and I descend
To Hades there to view,
What was, amid lost Shades who moan despair.

The Grey Light

Half-light floods the sleeping village now;
All is silent in September's dawn,
As night clouds wither where the light has torn
An eastern entrance, on yon hills low brow.

The wet slates glisten in enduring grey
And no smoke rises from the ash-dead fires.
Morning wakens, sleep-wrapt night retires,
To give to life again what gifts it may.

In these nights no frosts have gathered yet
But dry leaves tremble, bound sometime to fall,
A few are yellow now and round the hall
The vine leaves like old cheeks, blush rouged regret.

They belong to yesterday and now discarding age
Will cast them to October's grasping gales.
In trepidation held as light's last tenure fails,
They wait till breezes swell, to gale hot rage.

Eternal seasons sweep me off like leaves,
Torn from life's twists and mad tormented storms;
Did I fulfil those dreams which yearning forms
Or did I tread that path, which most deceives.

Soon dusk must come and give the village rest,
Small souls will snuggle in their beds to dream:
Of what may lie within fate's shadowed scheme
Before they entertain that final guest.

Beware my Friend Beware

Leaves weave yellow as days slow mellow
But beware my friend, beware!
Soon autumn's beauty says summer's duty
Is fulfilled, yet have a care
For — as sun sinks, dying, hear swallows sighing
As they turn to warmer air.

Soft mists caressing rich gathered threshings,
Mark the harvest of this year.
Yet it brings delusion that god's profusion
Will evermore be there.
Though the gift is given, will its terms imprison?
In a farscape, barren, bare.

In twilight creeping, those young heads sleeping
Must inherit what we dare.
This paradise by our device
May become some demon lair!
Drink your moment friend for as these days end,
Will the foul replace the fair?

Ode to Autumn

Pink-flame-burnt-edged hawthorn leaves
Now wither to decline;
Those restless winds October brings
Proclaim the end of time.
For death comes with November
To curse my woodland glades;
Where luscious green, midsummer's garb,
To lifeless yellow fades.
For leaves have autumn fever
And rot with black-spot now,
While others burn in scarlet robes,
Strewn down the bare hedgerow.

The plough has scarred the stubbled field,
Its clays stand sodden, brown,
And evensong calls down those shades
Which form pale winter's gown.
For in those mists lie memories:
Those ghosts of long ago,
Of love and laughter, joy and youth
Of loss and black sorrow.

More conscious in this season
Of my mortality.
I breathe the beauty of decay
Yet sense eternity.
Half sentient I slow sojourn
Completing my life's task;
Enriched once more by autumn's pain:
What more could dreamer ask?

The Fox

I took the shears to free the fox!
  There is no God, there is no God!
Its leg was rigid, red with blood,
  Locked, in silent pain.

It turned and softly snarled and looked;
  I cut the wires and leg unhooked
And pulled them from the burning flesh.

It looked, in thanks? Then weary lay
  Along a tree hid from the road
And weary, there remained.

Some food laid out — ignored or scorned,
  The water taken was not touched;
My offered help: disdained.

I went again, with salve to sooth
  To heal imagined agony;
The fox had gone and lay, somewhere?
  In cover, licking wounds to heal.

  Or so I hope, those knowing eyes
Still haunt me; had I not chanced by
  My brother would in torment hang,
There thirsting, as it slowly died.

I took my shears and freed a fox
  There is no God, there is no God!
My tortured soul dreams of Christ's blood,
  Locked in silent pain!

Forever

Forever through dying-dear autumn,
All things fit rightly in place,
For its stillness begets such high beauty
And its silence gives days of low grace.

Perhaps the wren's heartbeat, quick darting,
Glimpsed through snatched windows of time:
Fulfils, or the bold robin perching
Puffing its red breast sublime.

Maybe just log smoke, safe curling
High in the old chimney nook:
Comforts, with mind dragons swirling
As deep in the fire's heart I look.

In fever some red leaves hang, burning,
In agony waiting to fall.
While pale leprous yellows drift, swooning,
Down into time's vasty hall.

In mourning the dark wood leans, sighing,
For spring, which May's green dreams began.
Now ragged last remnants, draped, drying:
Remind all how soon life is done.

For the loan which youth takes, subsidising,
Wild nights, where eternal love plays,
Is forgotten, till come long years striding:
To claim what is owed, in short days!

But now in my dying-dear autumn
All things fit, rightly, in place
For the stillness begets such high beauty
And the silence gives days of low grace.

Broken Biscuits

Crumpled leaves lie dry and brown
Like broken biscuits on the lawn.
Some — lime and lemon, still to fall,
On flowering cherry hang, forlorn.

The northern breeze brings cheerless chills,
Where once rich flowers in riot bloomed;
There, where birthing filled the wood
Now dies a fading year, entombed.

Where are the songs of summer now?
Oh where is that spirit blithe and gay,
Lamenting through these dismal days,
Enshrouded in mist-wraiths of grey?

These are the months when hours drag slow
Through feeble remnants of the light;
When sunless aeons swallow time
And we are children of the night.

Oh for the turning of the year,
To see the snowdrops signal spring;
Then feel the warming of the world
And joy at new life wakening.

Emilia's Sonnet

Dusky daylight drifts towards its end
And breath of autumn stills, expecting night.
Now midge-crowd congregations swirl and wend
About some point unseen, in turmoiled flight.
These transient choirlings bring a darkling world
To hymn warm evening groves with silent song.
Through golden days October sinks, unfurled,
To frost nights where these motes no longer throng.
Above our Lych-gate path, with conkers strown
In burnished chaos, mid their spiky shells;
A log fire with its kind warmth waits at home
But now we roam where twilight's beauty dwells.
    For me, soon winter calls to pass its gate,
    For you spring's garlands and bright summer wait.

Solipsism

This is my heaven!
This is my hell!
This is my Cosmos!
This is my cell!

All in the mind
Is pleasure and pain;
I could seek surcease
But what would that gain?

Philosophers, Priests:
Their faint shadows see
As fragments of dreams
In some mystery.

I brood amid demons;
Lost in the night,
Like Satan I dwell
Expelled from the light.

Dead Season's Ghosts

Blow! Blow! — dead season's ghosts
And in your passing leave a tear.
Fall! Fall! — you sombre leaves,
Wrap rich decay around my year.

Writhe! Writhe! — you passing souls
And say farewell to this tired sun.
Wing! Wing! — to waiting realms
For in death's dreams new hopes are won

Tired days! Days! — those pallid dregs
Lived out like some last sigh
Of Love! Love! — which burned and raged
Through torrid nights, which saw it die.

Blow! Blow! — dead season's ghosts
Down from the tree called memory,
Pile low! Low! — on this year's grave
For all that's left is ennui.

The Lych-gate

In brooding shade, assemble swart old stones;
Above them rough hewn beams and crooked tiles.
In past times there new coffins, briefly, paused;
Till carried from that ancient second shroud.

Are memories retained there of old years?
Of solemn faces, farewells and regrets.
Your slow eroding centuries remind
The pain of being in our endless now:
Most thankfully in time's vast flow is brief.
For like those denizens of far off Thebes
Or Babylon or Tyre or mighty Rome
Our shadows pass as though we had not been.

Ephemeral joys your shadowed walls have held,
Rosebud brides, with ages past, long gone;
And spotless babes, now aged, stained with sin
Who wait their turn to face their reckoning;
If you believe, of course, that sort of thing.

'The rest is silence;' here amid these slabs,
Which unlike martial graves, stern ranked, elsewhere,
Stand all-angled — celebrate indiscipline,
For entropy must grow within the grave.
And sentinel to entry, none may leave,
Still stands this silent witness to the world:
The Lych-gate knew them all.

Strange and Rich

Strange and rich is autumn's season,
Corruption blights life's golden stream;
Life greets death — yet gives no reason.

Sad September's rich laid foison,
Of decadence, there ripe fruits teem;
Strange and rich is autumn's season.

Light lies vanquished by night's treason,
Banished, till comes vernal green;
Life greets death but gives no reason.

Black and scarlet drupes hang brazen
In decaying ripeness seen;
Strange and rich is autumn's season.

Nightshade flaunts its berries: poison,
Tempting taste-me-colours scream!
Life greets death yet gives no reason.

All must pass beyond orison,
Vanish, as midsummer's dream
Strange and rich is autumn's season;
Life greets death yet gives no reason.

Ode to Eternity

I mourn the solstice. Then, time bathes in light,
Forever hovers on midsummer's haze;
That moment marks the start of all decline
When perfect days give way to dying's time.
When soulful beauty like the rarest wine
Intoxicates the senses with regret;
For here is life's fulfilment and its end.

In anguished hymns or hollow metaphor
The poets try to see within the core
Of great creation; I can do no more.

Ethereal beauty of the dawn!
Dusk's purple splendour calling night!
Ice haloes round the haunted moon;
These sights soon lost to me.

That scent of spring when life is born!
Youth's mad carousing till the light!
Love's low ecstatic moans;
All, nevermore for me.
Exigent hours press down on me
So little time! So little time!

What moment does the heart begin to ache?
When swifts are gone?
With mellowing of the sun?
When luscious green turns dry?
This gentle time, when ripeness grows
And softly falls the fading rose:
Its beauty lingers turning to despair.

Loneliness now overwhelms:
Just emptiness remains;
As in schoolrooms where soft dust motes drift
Through empty holidays,
Or, on beaches long bereft of joyful young.
These are those times of wind-whipped-weeping shores,
Deserted miles of sand and sorry gales.
No longer azure emptied skies grow cold,
Their colour now: ice blue as a Viking eye.
Old paint peels on the silent carousel
And shutters flap, in monotone lament.

Bedraggled seaweed thoughts wrap round my mind.
This is the wistful world of fond regrets,
Brought with the sense of, fading ebbing years.

Now with the first cold winds come ancient fears
Of endless death lived in eternal night.
The fires of Hell are welcoming and warm:
Compared to lonely silence locked in ice!

Yet somewhere in this vacuum of decay,
This great lacuna when the psyche mourns,
Are compensations, which might yet restore?

Leaves whipped along in careless flight,
Star points in the velvet night,
Log warming redness from the fire,
The sense of one with life entire
Which time's rich flow must soon conspire
To bring a wished for ending to life's dream,
And show what autumn's dying riches mean.

Aubade

Aurora stands a tiptoe on reaching for the dawn
Her rosy fingers eastward steal to greet a day newborn.
Queen Mab's nightlight, called the moon, is snuffed and put away
As one by one the waking birds begin to have their say.
A veil of mist hung, ghostly, low, creeps slow across the fields
Wraith swirling whorls sink slow to bed as dark to daylight yields.
The meadow's shadowed hollows fill with gold as Sol's first rays
Dash through my avenue of oaks, to waken groaning clays.
Once Druids stood to greet that light; those mysteries are past!
Time mocks as old religions fall: that great iconoclast!
But now is now! My spirit fills with rapture at the sight,
The reincarnate world I greet with pagan pure delight.
No longer grey the limestone wall reflects that ancient fire,
Almost alive the old stone glows, as drunk with youth's desire.
A shy breeze flits from westward with delicate finesse
In promise of the Sun's return, she warms with each caress.
Imagined Pan-pipes haunt the wood and echo from the hill,
And bright once more the world reborn each heart with hope must fill.

Yet I am of the evening and soon must journey on
To ponder lost millennial dreams with Troy and Babylon.
Those death filled eyes once drank each dawn, in love with life as I.
They long have passed all pain and lust as I will, by and by.

In youth we were immortal, yet tell that to the years
Inexorably moving on, for none they shed their tears.
Now as I breathe the frost-fresh air each sense finds new employ;
Existence builds of moments: a few we may enjoy.
This one is such, thus sings my soul in innocence again;
The cynic, momently, is fled — my boyhood I regain.
Though now at last the magic's past and morning must begin
I'll lightly tread life's road today, and joy in journeying.

Minimalist Villanelle

Sun low
Red leaves
Shadows grow

Gales blow
November eves
Sun low

Mist slow
Dusk weaves
Shadows grow

Scraggy Crow
Homeward leads
Sun low

Hedgerow
Crimson bleeds
Shadows grow

Sorrow
Autumn breeds
Sun low
Shadows grow

Out with the Dogs

While out with the dogs at the end of night
A soot finger of cloud pointed east, to the light;
All was silent and still in my autumn mood,
I walked with the gods and my solitude.

By some trick of the mind from the path I was gone
To Troy where I fought with a Myrmidon,
Hence to sip wine with old Khayyam
Who said: "like a rose in the desert is man."
From there at warp ten to a Nova star
To watch as it blew off its outer layer.
Then with the Buddha 'neath his Bodhi tree,
To ask could we fools know reality?
Last, I juggled with quarks at a proton's core
And turned lead to gold as a quick encore.

I woke from my dream with a sudden start
And all of my visions had gone from the park,
The dogs chased a hare going quite berserk
I walked home and shaved, then set off for work.

Lords and Ladies

With finery of Lords and Ladies gone
Putrescent orange berries now remain;
My drying, dying, wood is nearly done,
Last leaves drink dreg-rays of a failing sun.

Their sickly near dead cousins wait to fall
Into great autumn, lying there to rot;
Amid corruption beauty lingers still
As daylight hovers under twilight's pall.

I witness this wild rapture of decay;
That charnel house: tomorrow, comes too soon.
The age of sorrows waits, yet not too long,
For all must dance last-dying's roundelay.

Life must be held in those eternal arms
Which banish sorrow, mock all fond regret,
Like some faded, bloodless, vampire bride
Seduced forever by sweet voiceless charms.

It seems the world must hold its precious breath,
Not daring to let go lest it release
The one who gathers all, yet none would choose
To go with him; that faceless one called Death.

Twilight of the Gods

Incredibly golden, bright, so bright,
Amid grey streaking cloud seen through autumn trees,
Dying the sun sheds the last of its light,
I stand on the hillside scarce daring to breathe,
Transfixed by this dying-light sent by the gods
I drink in the vision no brush could repeat,
All comes together, with no part at odds.
This is pure beauty my soul is replete.
The breeze seems to hush as twilight steals around,
Gold becomes purple as day takes its flight,
Velvet long fingers creep over the ground
Closing the circle as day becomes night.
    My spirit soars, such memories are won
    To light that darkness which so soon must come.

Transmutation

The equinox is passed and sombre autumn,
Frowning, browns the earth beneath the plough;
Leaves are falling, paying winter's ransom
And with their dying deck the wood-paths now
With rich sepulchral colours of decay.
Fevered reds are laid with wasting yellows,
Mottled ambers ooze a last display;
Soon they fall into their coffined hollows,
Sere and silent, laid in vast arrays,
Waiting for their final transmutation
To elementals freed to go their ways:
Above, buds wait reincarnation.
    These dying hues remind that we decline
    Our lives, like leaves, are swept away by time.

The Wine is Almost Gone

Lamps turned low give out an amber glow,
The singer sings lost love from deep within:
Soliloquies of sorrow born of age;
I drift within her mood: dissatisfied.
Memories, like flickers of old flames
Stir from ashes burnt out long ago,
Phantoms, fanned to life by Ennui.

Faces, voices, thoughts, dissolve and change
Amid this fog of depressed reverie
To other, fabled, younger, brighter nights
When we lay close before a blazing fire
All-contents, with nothing but youth's hope.

Now I live this meaningless charade,
Amid the wealthy plump self satisfied;
Boozy, in black tie and gold brocade:
Those ritual markers of our middle age.

Alas, for all the candle burns one way;
I am trapped in time: October man
Gone forever is youth's sacred rage.

The music fades, the singer bows and turns
Polite applause moves with her from the stage.
I too must leave: part of the worn out night,
The dream is dreamed, the wine is almost gone.

Labyrinthine Years

Age bestows acceptance and a sadness;
Mellower those passions which still rage,
Gone quicksilver youth with its brief madness
Yet much remains before I quit life's stage.
The mirror shows some greying and odd wrinkle
Yet eyes still sparkle in that image there;
Shoulders strong, yet waist becoming ample
Not fat but somehow thicker year by year.
Still I feel the restlessness of springtime
And autumn's vivid beauty sears my soul.
Still I seek some meaning to life's dark-rhyme;
Where reason damns, a poets dreams console.
 Through life's labyrinthine years I seek my grail
 To journey well is all: though all must fail.

Ghosts

Down the silent path in the closing dark
I walk the dogs tonight.
Near the graveyard wall falls a shadowed pall
Marked in cold and ghastly light.

Did a shadow move, did my eyes just prove
What the rational mind must fear?
In the convent grove does some spirit rove
Or a watchful fox creep near.

Now I lift the dogs and then vault the wall
To a world of yesteryear,
Where the Abbe lies with faint Jobs and Janes
Stretching back to — who knows where?

For here Saxons built and the Romans camped
But the legions long are gone,
Yet on summer nights when the south breeze wafts
I hear their 'Mithras' song.

How dark the church with its memoried stone,
Now I skirt its towered bend,
Do dark shapes flit, or Hobgoblins sit,
On that leaning gravestone's end?

Soon comes Halloween, with its spirits loosed
While the sun has lost its power,
Then compelled they sink to the underworld
As the rose-dawn starts to flower.

At the old Lych-gate I dare not wait:
Here the lonely coffins pause,
Amid sighs and tears and regrets and fears
At the unknown's open doors.

None may forego this last journey slow
Which leads to rest, in earth.
In that final home where all love is done,
We lie long, embraced by earth.

Now I pass the gate and the dogs pull hard
For such is their delight
To sniff and growl at the things which prowl
Down the byways of the night,
Whether ghost or owl or monk in cowl
With tormented eyes, from hell,
Or mouse or vole, startled from its hole
By some spectral midnight bell.

I feel them near by some mind sense, queer,
From our eldritch days long gone;
Some would laugh or sneer, they might mock to hear
At such nonsense, held by one,
Who in logic deals, yet some power reveals —
Gives a sense that just maybe
There are more things in heaven and earth
Than in your philosophy!

Nowhere-to-go Wind

You kick the leaves around purposely
Like a small boy booting a can.
You buffet the windows and rattle the tiles
In a bored and pointless fashion;
You momentarily expire and then revive,
Dodging around with renewed vigour
Seeking something useful to do;
But late in the year you are just a nuisance
With nowhere much to go.

Your cousins woke the earth,
Bringing the spring rains
To satisfy the yearning of the fields.
In summer you sighed and dried the wheat
Towards harvesting.
In September you swelled the fruits
And then beautified October
With swirls of death coloured leaves.

But by November you are pretty much at a loose end
And really not much use for anything.
Thus, while we sit inside,
Cosy and warm through the long nights,
You, you poor thing, are locked out alone in the cold;
No wonder we hear you moaning in the night.

Haiku of the Autumn Months

Hints of endings now
Mists – heavy fruits – cleansing rain
Yet such forebodings

Such painful beauty
Oh the colours of your leaves
Dying's coronal

Soon all hallows eve
Hags let loose the fiends of night
Vanquishing the light

As this world withers
Despair rides autumn's shadow
Through bleak December

Lost Love's Reverie

The moon looks down with watery eye
On fields where autumn veils foretell:
Soon comes the hour when lovers sigh
And taste that poignant draught: farewell.

Soft hours swift sped on rapture's spurs
To fill the halls of memory,
For when mind roams through those empty years,
In thrall to lost love's reverie.

Autumn Brocade

Now, in full glory, the leaves turn around
Assuming the rich hues of mourning.
Some like spent embers lie, cold, on the ground;
Others high hung in the boughs are still burning.
Oak, birch and elm all shed their golden rain,
Beech woods pour bronzes October has made
Flooding with copper each dry ditch and drain;
Sweeping down banks filling pathway and glade.
Sorrel cascades, with dull dun drifting free;
All join the motley the night breeze has laid.
Though dying the year my heart cheers to see
Its winding sheet woven in autumn brocade.
    Oh the colours of the leaves this year!
    Their raging splendour warns that winter's near.

Wild flung amongst the Wheat

Sultry July; when lost-forever-hours drift by,
Like lazy clouds.
Post orgasmic, spent, we lie,
Mirroring the torpid afternoon,
Heavy languor drugs the day
As summer's perfume fills the shaded room.

> *Lush nectar fills the flower*
> *Full blossomed grows the rose*
> *The bee sips hour by hour*
> *Her drone hymns our repose.*

With shallow breath the breeze licks fevered flesh —
Cooling erotic fires
Which flamed as bodies twined like liquid eels
And eager softness captured muscled steel
Until excruciating pleasure at love's peak;
Then slow release, descending into blankness.

> *Through air-vaults, azure, deep*
> *Swallows arc on high,*
> *Mare's tails wisp the sky*
> *Scarce moving as we sleep.*

In limpid eddies coital pleasures fade
And lovers drowse, serene;
Eyes which glowed with urgent hot desire
Are blank and hyalescent, hypnotised,
Insensate, lost where silent currents flow
Down torrents in loves sensuous undertow.

> *Wild flung among the wheat*
> *The crimson poppies blow*
> *Their fume drifts on the heat*
> *Of mid-day, nodding slow.*

Our transient tempest: maelstrom of delights
Is spent for now.
Yet from narcotic lassitude of day
Comes carnal Night
Whose subtle darkness velvetly conspires
To whet once more desires keen appetite.

By the meadowsweet
Soft drying grasses blow
All life seems idle slow
Wrapt in the mid-day heat.

This world's rich opulence is ripe
For sensual taking.
Voluptuousness abounds,
Dark, fecund, aching,
Inviting, in abandon joy,
New making!

Shades glide and evening's chill
Draws mist-wraiths from the lake,
Now Pan stirs on the hill
And Venus starts to wake.

Nature claims us for her own,
We must obey her strict imperative:
'This is your hour, combine to make new life,
Which time from you is taking!'
Poor marionettes compelled, dance while you may
Ecstatic to life's oldest roundelay.

Now autumn brings decline
Life's harvest is complete,
Now I lie replete
With loves sweet wine.

Autumn, Summer, Winter

There's a rage in the heart of autumn
In this perfect solitude
As though time regrets that it's slow neglect
Might spoil this interlude.

For the days, compelled, grow shorter
And the arctic winds must come,
To where starving birds seek shelter,
Yet the dying year gives none.

Now the copse must stand in ruin
Through the barren months dismay;
What once was clothed in realms of light
Stands in mourning — grey!

Yet what of you my lovely girl,
The ripening fills your womb;
Live through your splendid summer now
Leave me to winter's gloom.

(Dawn was heavily pregnant with Emilia when I wrote this.)

Golden October

Golden October, Sunday afternoon,
Sun drenched languid beauty lingers still,
As warm light bathes low banks, where all too soon
Blown leaves will heap to choke the winding rill.
Soon by the copse a plough will brow the earth,
And turn the stubble, marking well the end
Of autumn's plenty, bringing winter's dearth,
For soon its icy darkness must descend.
Yet now my wooded halls are full of light,
With trees lit, splendid, in their yellow gowns
Decay is marked in colours of delight,
Which now this fading season briefly loans.
    In beauty's shades a dying year departs
    With memories of its splendour in our hearts.

Vapour Trails
Seen from Thorpe in Balne

Wisp-cloud is brushed in whorls around a sun
Half sunk amid its cloudy couching hills;
Where nacreous streams in dusk-swirled eddies run
Towards a night drawn down those fragile rills.
Seven jets, mark out slow brush strokes in the sky,
Those trails lead everywhere a mind could go;
Amid tree fronds of autumn, watching, I
Squat crab-like in my earth bound pool below.
Joy and sadness mingle in my mood,
Thoughts rise on where they sail those silver wings;
While I am chained below condemned to brood
Cursed by those shadows which each dark night brings.
    The east grows bleak and chills my heart with cold
    While westward, sunset dreams of summer's gold.

Amber

There is something about autumn light,
Beauty descends with its gloom
Like amber enfolding the night

To take the world's cares from my sight
Its soft, subfusc, shadows enwomb,
There is something about autumn light.

When equinox gales loose their might
Umber thoughts with the short days resume,
Like amber enfolding the night.

Memories of soft candlelight
Flicker like ghosts round the room,
There is something about autumn light.

In its arms love and I reunite
And regret long lost dreams importune
Like amber enfolding the night.

Now death's season my senses excite
As it beauty emotions consume
There is something about autumn light
Like amber enfolding the night.

Minimalist Sestina

Autumn leaves
Dying thronging
All descend
Immortal longing
Beauty grieves
All must end.

All must end
Autumn leaves
Beauty grieves
Dying thronging
Immortal longing
All descend.

All descend
All must end
Immortal longing
Autumn leaves
Dying thronging
Beauty grieves.

Beauty grieves
All descend
Dying thronging
All must end
Autumn leaves
Immortal longing

Dying thronging
Immortal longing
All must end
Beauty grieves
All descend
Autumn leaves.

Immortal longing
All descend
Dying thronging
Beauty grieves
All must end
Autumn leaves.

Immortal longing
All must end
All descend

The Muse

The muse is upon me,
So late in the night
Wild with that willed
Unwilling, I write.
Spurred by some spectre
Dark truths to reveal;
Do spirits un-shrived
The unholy conceal?

All-hallow's eve:
Old phantoms arise
Taunting — fool write
While yet you have eyes,
Swiftly, you burn
With passionate fires —
Know death's lake of shadows
Must drown all desires.

But now! Forced; unwilling;
To write I must go,
My muse is upon me
I dare not say no.

The Viking
A narrative from Days of old

The Viking gazed from out his halls
His eyes had dimmed, his hands were gnarled;
Though winter's death had chilled his bones
His far look went where youth had roamed.

He thought of wars and many things,
Of memories which long life brings.
There stood honour: stained; he'd tried!
For nature wills, its laws decide
On which paths we venture down,
Who we will cross, what loves we're thrown.

Through green-grey eyes he drank the moon
Soft gliding through eternal gloom.
He felt its chill despite the fire,
That ennui of dead desire
Which comes with heimal cold and age
When passion's flames no longer rage.

He felt that power of shoulders broad
Which come to those who use the sword
Or spear or axe, to win with blood
A space for those his heart would love.

He stared in silence, felt no fears
Of what would vanish with the years.
He knew man's life which came unseen
Would go: the shadow of a dream.

What prayers there are bring small relief
To those who cling to veiled belief,

Such cowering moans are not for me:
I roam the paths of destiny,
To taste what strange existence gives
What loves it loans, which deeds it sieves
Before we pass beyond the dusk
To join all dreams, forgotten dust.

The sun stands pale, low in the day,
The nights are long, my thoughts are grey;
My heart is frozen like the snow,
How I would welcome ending now.

Then; as I looked amid the trees
Wild emeralds gleamed dark mysteries
A she-wolf, brief, returned my gaze
Her eyes flame-faithful, unafraid.
Her soul was free, her scent was strong
She did not brood on right or wrong.
Her life moved down old hidden ways
Unmoved by hopes which age betrays.

She did not covet afterlife
What comes will come through death's sharp knife.
To live life's rage is all she cares
Untrammelled by belief's pale snares.
Her ancient wisdom drinks 'the now',
Its joys and sorrows through her flow.

Fierce in desire to shield her own
From traps, with which the world is strewn.
She stood in beauty strong of soul
But something lacked to make her whole.

I heard her sighing through the trees
Come let us mingle destinies.
I hesitated, looked behind,
Then strode beyond all humankind.
The she-wolf howled and instinct cried
An answer, or my heart had lied.

I reached a clearing mid old oaks
But she had vanished, gone like smoke.
In her place that mystery —
The temptress who had summoned me.

"Enchantress dark, I heard your cry:
A plea my power could not deny."
She said: "you know why I have come
Our souls have touched, we move as one."

I called; "and look our route is there
For we must leave to reach — nowhere.
So short is life, but there is time
To go and taste that thing sublime;
My body, soul, I freely give
For time within your heart to live."

Her lips I tasted: oh such wine!
Her eyes compelled, though she was mine.
And I was hers, beyond belief,
Her perfumed pleasures would not cease.
Once, long ago I felt this pain
And vowed it would not come again.

Yet in that rapture of desires
I burned once more in love's wild fires.
My oath had melted in that heat
Which comes when wolf and she-wolf meet.

The Velvet Time

Clouds drift high in moonlit sky,
Then slip beyond the trees
And I hear that near dawn minstrelsy
Of silence and unease,
Which clasps me tight in claws of night
In my world of hope and fear,
As I ride once more that ecstasy
Which the hidden world brings near.

In this velvet time come those thoughts — sublime
Which can reach the far beyond,
To that quantum-cosmos mystery;
Do I see some guiding hand?
In forbidden realms amid core-chained quarks
Or dark matters secret maze
Are the gods locked up in this secret place?
Or none! Till end of days.

At three Kelvin hiss the unending kiss
Of creation, slow to die.
Where the chaos cooled, to form destiny:
Wherein no answers lie.
From the atom's core to the birth of light
Deep patterns tantalise;
Here I feel that promised wonderment
Which certainty denies.

Pagan Music

Come play! Send sudden shivers amid the turning leaves
O rise you autumn spirits! Breathe, restless round my eaves.

Ripe hips to rose-red, burning, and kiss the russets gold;
My year for end is yearning, its summer flame grows cold.

Come fill the woods with scarlet and berries: purple, black,
Let death resume dominion and take his fiefdom back.

His dyings paint such beauty among these gnarled hedgerows
And through his gate waits freedom, released amid its throes.

Come drink decay's rich colours, which riot through the mind
And hear that pagan music which yet haunts humankind.

For our souls grow in the meadow, near brooks and leafy glades
And wither in that wilderness which wilful greed has made.

The Moon

The moon is the colour of death tonight!
I feel cold fingers clutch my heart.
Time dissolves within a dream:
Perhaps this autumn I'll depart.

Slithering days crawl to their holes
Which open at the edge of night;
Then I see those midnight ghouls
Which gnaw my sanity till light.

Winter's chill has come so early,
Amid leaves burning red and gold;
The lyric of its song sounds dreary:
Come find what non-existence holds.

Lichen

Only the lichen on the rocks
Only the wind-howl: raw,
Are oblivious to those sentient shocks
Which torment what we are.

For how we pose and what we seem
Are, thinnest, thin veneer.
We are those dancers in that dream
Drawn dark by — Hamlet; Lear.

Existence is the strangest thing,
Its whirlpool sucks me down,
To where the joy of death might bring
Solace within his gown.

Only the lichen on the rocks
Only the wind-howl raw
Are insensate to life's running clocks
Which chime at nevermore.

Elsewhere

I have a sense of restless life elsewhere
From those who write of cities: which I hate!
Of sweating subways filled with rushing souls
In lifts, down stairs, to multi-varied goals.
These are closed-glass and concrete-heaving-hells
Which crowd me close, infringing my small space,
I need old woods, sweet meadows; quiet days,
The knife-wind's kiss on dark deserted fells.

Some crave the hub and bub of full cafés
A South Bank or a Greenwich Village crowd;
Attentive throngs to throw the ego food;
But I must lone-wolf down lost-lovely ways
Where un-distracted I can listen loud
To that voice within — of solitude.

Dionysus

Who frees the Bacchant from her chains
Gives licence to an older lore—
In glades where fear and bloodlust reigns.

Dionysus, wild, with flowing mane
Lets loose those ruled by fang and claw—
To dance in darkness; half insane.

The thyrsus* guides through reason's bane
To where the slave-chaste-flesh, before—
Was held in place by guilt and shame.

Thus bonds of duty rip and strain
Then break to free the being's core—
Which would its ancient roots regain.

The baneful moon with her cold flame,
Mocks, while instinct free and raw
Gives licence to an older lore,
In glades where fear and bloodlust reigns.

---

* thyrsus: ivy covered wand, with which Bacchants beat the
ground during Dionysian orgies.

Ode Autumnal

October's days have wandered past
Down paths half-filled with wretched leaves;
Black spotted plague gripped fellows cast
To ground, blown round my gale whipped eaves.
There scarlets burn, mid yellows pale
Where toadstools prosper, deathly white;
The year must sleep, soon winter's veil
From dawn to dusk will dim the light.

In cloying whorls drift wraiths of mist
Amid cold clays which steel has scarred;
The plough-blade, weary earth has kissed
And golden rows of stubble marred.
September's gypsy days are lost!
So brief those fading weeks, sublime;
Soon fruit filled hedge turns bare and frost
Will sculpt my dells with hoary rime.

When swallows flee how days decline
For demon night is loosed to feast
And hold the world in ransomed time,
Until spring wakes and brings release.

Death's henchman then all joy denies
And I must grieve for loved things gone:
A word, a look, for faithful eyes,
For thoughts too late and deeds undone.

Yet small, defiant, pure and clear
I hear a robin in full tune;
That herald of the coming year
Sings: spring will vanquish all your gloom;
Soon snowdrops come and crocus blues
Which promise feasts of longer days,
And with them vibrant life-fresh hues
To free these doom enshrouded ways.

Dusk

My evening starts amid old trees
As darkness seeps between brown leaves,
And wraps in black huge barren boughs
And inks the glades as twilight grows.

A high last blue now fades to grey,
Mid western embers of the day
Of straw and glory-golden red
As Sol sinks wearily to bed.

Then velvet curtains of the night
Shut out last remnants of the light,
And diamond points grow one by one
As afterglow's last rays are done.

Past midnight now, a ghost-ship moon
Leaves a wake of silver gloom;
In shadowed veils all lights last gleam
Is banished to foul night's demesne.

The Last Days

Stubble runs in flaxen rows
Down slopes where lazy sunlight glows,
And restless time now hardly flows.

Soon slews the plough then gold gives way
To coruscations in the clay:
From ochre red to corpse like grey.

These dregs of summer gently fade
While swallows gather: farewells made,
To garnered field and ripened glade.

The moon hangs mellow, nights are warm
Soon comes the dying, then the turn,
Until from despond spring is born.

Mischief

Here earth is woken by the beauteous dawn
And kissed so softly by the setting sun.
At dusk there is a candle lit against the darkness
With spirits of the wild wood now adjured
To be the guardians of this sacred place.

Around about the breeze sighs its lament
A mourning yew weeps tears of silent dew,
Above, the silver birch stands tall: a sentinel.

Below, deep in the grief-hewn rock, secure;
With him, a teddy bear and chocolate buttons and his
        Rawhide chew.
Between his paws as he liked,
Daring you to try to take it,
His bone shaped biscuit.

Here he will lie, dreaming through eternity
Cradled lovingly in his basket.

Merry

Merry has his good earth bed
Laid at his brother's side,
In basket wrapped with tiny bear
To spend his eventide.

When young he trotted down the lane
With head raised looking round
And looked in wonder at the world,
Till safe, there he was found.

Mischief as the madcap sped
Whilst he the steadfast, who
Would follow where his leader led
With sniffing work to do.

And I at least have memories
Of him beside the fire
In slumber deep stretched with that ease
Which all-contents desire.

For fifteen years within my heart
They dwelled those doggy souls
Though sadness clouds long days apart:
That love we shared consoles.

Smudge

Tiny Smudge, ill when he came
From breeders with no souls
Was shy and hid, afraid of sounds
And ate those crumbs he stole.

But patient kindness saw him grow
And gain what dogs are owed.
A warm safe bed laid at our feet
With love on him bestowed.

And now the wilful terror rules
Through hours of endless play
And in the evening's stroked and spoiled,
Content at end of day.

The Golden Leaves

Now my psyche drinks disturbéd winds,
Low mists, which gentle earth to rich decline.
These are the days when velvet evening wins
and life must join the detritus of time.
Old loves, which bring such pain, must sink to rest,
Claimed by that law which takes the golden leaves;
Though all must go, these days at my behest
Linger in beauty while my spirit grieves.
Soon comes the time when winter's demon stalks
Through barren woods, so soulless, stripped of joy;
Poisoned those paths down sodden woodland walks,
Till reborn light returns: sweet spring's envoy.
    Reflection on what's been, what is to be
    Mingle regret with fondest memory.

The Stillness

A new moon drifts so lazily amid the whispen grey,
The sun has set and golden dusk ending to my day.
The air is clear and frost garbed imps await the midnight call
To sculpt my lawn with icy fronds beneath night's velvet pall.

Now darkness fills the brooding wood for summer's glow is gone,
The little death of winter comes for harvest joys are done.
The watchful vixen seeks her prey for times will soon be lean
And softer eyes are careful now, for they must not be seen.

Leaves pile high in mouldering mounds as coverings for graves
For Augusts' warmth is buried here amid stark winter's staves.
Life's vital spark lies dormant now within November's tombs
Until springs herald trumpets hope and vanquished light resumes.

Another year has passed my way, from catkins till last rose
And friends seem gathered one by one unto their last repose.
For now, alone, I journey on, awhile at least it seems,
Until that autumn when I'll rest amid eternal dreams.

Symphony of the Leaves

Leaves cascade down in wild colours flavours,
Scarlets and yellows: November is near;
A visual largo whose crochets and quavers
Are hymned by the eye and not by the ear.

Now where thin wet mists, lick the trees in the morning
Lie new cadenzas, the night wind has blown,
New beauty has fallen from dusk till the dawning
Telling a year that its tenure has flown.

Requiems rise — black spotted, sickly,
Arabesques twirl dressed in russet and rose
This melody penned in hues scattered fickly
A chaotic cantata of final repose.

Forlorn lie these codas in tunes lost forever,
This requiem riot can never reprise.
Walk soft through this beauty for soon endless never
Will fold itself round you, like yesteryear's leaves.

Villanelle of the Styx

I approach death's shadowed gates
On my journey to the Styx:
Fair haired Rhadamanthys waits!

Long past are loves and hates,
Here gloom and twilight mix,
I approach death's shadowed gates.

Past mending: your mistakes
Ever locked in time's matrix:
Fair haired Rhadamanthys waits!

Your life ends, decree the fates
You must enter realms of Nyx
Far beyond death's shadowed gates.

What you lived — no lie negates
Here truth is testatrix.
Fair haired Rhadamanthys waits!

Now Charon navigates
All is done, you glide transfixed
Through death's shadowed gates,
Where Rhadamanthys waits.

The Changeling Woods

I am not from a place of ancient wild grandeur,
Where cloud rivers boil over lowering peaks.

My heart does not seek that vast towering splendour,
Where eternal tides rage against wave torn harsh cliffs.

Though bleak moors have beauty spread through the high yonder,
Where black rocks stand guard above purpling haze.

I belong where the elf-stolen changeling woods are,
Where brook slivers slip through my green-sleeved dark glades.

In decline I will gladly, my fading days squander
Down those autumn-mist ways where my youth's wilding ran.

Tea in a Torquay Hotel

Tea in a Torquay hotel:
Which smelled of old pearls and decay,
With manners as stiff
As the doors on the lift,
Made of iron in a pre-thirties way.

The music was light, middle brow,
Insipid, not hurting the ears;
How I longed for the clang
Of Rock's raucous twang
Or bombastic Beethoven's loud sneers.

In atmosphere, ossified, quaint
I drank in the scene, like old malt;
The clerk at the desk
Was pure Betjemanesque,
A relic! But was that his fault?

Let some go abroad if they will
To those flies and that garlicy smell,
But let me live the dream
With hot scones, clotted cream,
At tea in a Torquay hotel.

Sonnet/Counter – Sonnet 1

At last have come those rich autumnal days
For golden wheat gives us its yield;
Beneath the mellow sun's slow drying haze
The stooks stand scythed and ready in the field.
Warm breezes kiss the dying drying grass
Whose seed may chance on fertile ground and grow,
The cycle thus renews infinitas
As autumn's endless harvests come and go.
Now, black and yellow humming while he works,
A bumble bee late burgles drooping flowers
His pollen must be saved for winter lurks:
Scarce three new moons release her awesome powers.

Eternal season's rhythms move along;
But lately, nature haunts me with her song.

What is my place among these riches seen?
By that which heaven-ward peers through time's vast door.
Which probes where quantum entities must teem?
In quark held dungeons at the atom's core.
Are we still of, or must we move beyond,
The beauty of our birthing planet: Earth?
If we remain we must keep Eden's bond
Or outcasts, on some new world seek rebirth!
Past boundless stars our restless eyes have roamed,
We must explore that universe vast sea!
Our childhood's gone! Arcadia was loaned!
Yet lingers in this autumn memory.

Sonnet/Counter – Sonnet 4

Soon must come those melancholy gifts
Of beauty as ripe fruits begin to fall.
Dewed cobwebs hang and ghostly morning mists
Enshroud my silent path with their soft pall.
Wild colours riot, vivid in my mind,
Dry leaves drip amber, sloes hang: carrion blue;
Fevered yellows, frenzied reds combine
To paint the wood in dying's every hue.
The hooded crow, so solitary, wings
Across bare fields straight scarred by furrows brown,
And lengthening shadows, sad, each new day brings
For winter soon must don her bridal gown.

Dark thoughts come with autumn's solitude,
Lately I have thought: what brings this mood?

The sadness of decline must conquer all!
None escapes from destiny's vast maze,
Macabre fate, invites to one last ball
To learn that dance of death which ends our days.
Yet we have lived and loved and should delight
That we have wrenched some meaning from the years;
Though sweet our day, soon comes that endless night
Whose gentle sleep must halt all pain, all tears.
Thus cease all sorrow, pay with joy all debt,
For that will cleanse you come eternity;
Greet well tomorrow, live with no regret
Each day well seized mocks pale futurity.

Languor

The languor of the dying sun
Sighs to the world of harvests won
—through golden autumn days.

In splendour now the turning leaves
Whisper, plucked by fretful breeze
—we fall to rest, ablaze.

The wonder of October's dawn;
Mists gentling those fields forlorn
—where once danced summer's haze.

Meandering through azure skies,
Swallows murmur last goodbyes
—then wend their sunward ways.

Loves must sunder, life must cease
What remains are memories
—which death cannot erase.

Keats and Shelley, revisited

Almost too painful are those memories I read
Of autumn idylls, vanished long ago.
Soft winnowed words conspire my heart to bleed,
For all youth's naive dreams are vanished now.

My mind's eye sees: a ruined cider-press,
Its oak hard frame sucked dry by wistful years;
Those last sweet oozing long ago were fresh,
As were those wonders our bright spirits shared.

There was a time; oh there was a time!
When like the Wild West Wind I seemed so free;
That briefest season, magical, sublime:
Yet only leased to us by destiny.

Now, my heart aches and a drowsy numbness pains
For I have drunk the hemlock of the years.
Of blushful Hippocrene, a draught perhaps remains
Before my glass is washed clean by death's tears.

Twilight

Ghosts hang, floating, gloating,
Upon dusk's heavy air,
With all of life declining
They watch the waning year
To see who steps through death's late opened door.

They are mere memories, echoed,
Beyond all thought or care:
Death dimensioned spectres,
To which, each wild November,
Gales pile wreaths at random,
To celebrate this season.

Souls sink, goodbying, dying,
For night comes everywhere;
What point regret's last sighing
Your shroud's weft is despair,
Its warp is timeless strands of nevermore.

Lost years ran where strong years flowed,
Down reckless weirs, to where?
May Lethe's streams protect us!
Do stagnant tarns remember
Those years when we were golden,
And loves un-shamed abandon?

What wraith comes sliding, gliding,
From some midnight lair.
Is this Sorrow, yearning —
All past hurts to repair?
But what's done is done, decrees time's law.

Each chose their lonely low road
From summer's glades so fair.
Where are its scents and nectars?
Amid this falling amber
Where only shadows beckon
To realms beyond orison.

Autumnal

The grass in the meadow is yellowing,
Renouncing its Juvenal green;
My year, past September, is mellowing
In tune with some rhythm unseen.

The wind in the willows is whispering
Of autumn, where sweet solitude
Hangs like the dawn's early mistening,
Enshrouding my pensive-dark mood.

Fading, the short days are scurrying
To ending amid the lost leaves;
There to fall when the death-winds are flurrying
To lie, where I'll long take my ease.

With the year past the equinox, hurrying,
Melancholic November's moon seems
To invite exeat from this worrying
And cares of life's shadowy dreams.

Styx

Now what awaits? We glide so slow, so slow!
Through mists and darkness, hear the river call,
To slaves compelled to glide within its thrall,
All must obey when called; none can say no.
Its icy vapours breathe the smell of death
Which fills the dank and deadly lifeless air.
Foul and fearsome Charon lingers there,
To ferry those descending from the earth
A silver Obol is the only fare.
The fee is cheap but is the journey dear?
The legends speak of peace and yet I fear
That which awaits beyond all toil and care.
    The oarsman calls and soon we must embark
    Beyond all knowing, into endless dark.

Acheron

Waters of sorrow lap that silent shore
Where those who think of loved ones seek to cross,
They seem to murmur 'think of nevermore',
Unable to return and mend their loss.
Here stagnant pools conceal regretful deeps
And reeds bend low and whisper — fretfully;
For no birds sing and dreadful quiet keeps
That gate which you must enter — wistfully.
These are those meres of ending and goodbye
Where love is lost amid eternal shade,
All hope is past, for none may now deny
What's done is done and here life's price is paid.
    Take one backward long and lingering glance,
    And then move on, a shadow in death's trance.

Lethe

Of sweet watered Lethe let me drink
That I might sleep, oblivious of time;
Into kind forgetfulness to sink,
To dream of soul dark beauties' rarest wine
Of waiting lips and soft seductive eyes,
Of languid nights forever in your arms,
Of days of laughter under silk blue skies,
Of wilful pleasure locked in loves wild storms.
I will not wander as a mournful shade
But find some stream kissed grove where I can muse
On those joys which came when close we laid,
In that world which all of us must lose.
    I do not worry; though all life must cease
    I'll make of Hades what I damned well please.

The Vigil of Sardonicus

Boreas pulls down last leaves now woods begin Novembering,
Bloodless day gives rise to night in this fast turning year;
And creaking joints inform the mind, there can be no dissembling:
Time for you is very short and ending must be near.

Deep within I'm seventeen! Who looks from the mirror there!
What fleshy face is moulded round those old and knowing eyes?
Who is that imposter who returns my youthful stare?
For I am spring and pleasuring but he looks near demise.

Protest all you like, poor fool! The Lords of Time stand beckoning,
Those seasons they allotted you must shortly disappear.
Did you think forever flamed your candle, short and guttering?
Soon death's draft will blow it out; let me make that clear!

You might in panic cast about to seek life's extra share
Seek for youth's elixir or believe some Shaman's lies.
No matter what, you'll cross the Styx and pay wild Charon's final fare,
Enjoy the rest of your short life but think on; how time flies!

Join with me in keeping well the Vigil of Sardonicus
Fill a glass, and yet drink deep devoid of hope or fear,
And wait to hear the awful chime which brings the last sleep over us,
Then queue to see what waits beyond — but stand right at the rear.

A Murder of Crows

A murder of crows wheels in the wind
For the day's solemn sky says that 'summer has sinned'.
Thus ripped from the year, sad autumn alone
In the colours of death must for summer atone.

In this season of mists, how yellow the leaves
Which are tugged by the gale and then drift on the breeze;
In vast heaps they lie now at dew-dismal-dawn.
Pale pawns in that gambit called life, laid forlorn.

With its fruits mostly gathered, yet some in decay
Hang waiting and crimson-swift-poisons display;
Still succulents, few, hang high in the trees,
Blue black over-ripe now, their flesh droops: diseased.

A fever is raging, mid lost hectic reds
Pursued by the west wind: as Shelley late said,
Till mouldering piles of dank rotting black
Moan with the groans of a year on the rack.

But time cannot rest and no thing can last,
I mark years by poets as seasons drift past;
Soon Winter the Huntsman rides his iron glade
As merciless hoar frost on life's end is laid.

The pagan world turns and the unconquered sun
Will swell after solstice, with New Year's begun
Spring's hounds at their traces are bound by shadows,
Hear the dying year's herald — A Murder of Crows!

These are the Times of the Dead

Now falls the glimmering light;
Greying and glowingly soft,
Laying to rest with the tiredness of time
A year, where the watchword is loss.

Rage, burns old leaves on the thorn.
Blood-berries drip to the ground.
Sallow and pale grows the floor of the wood
With dread emptiness scattered around.

Soon comes the poison-silk-night,
Cold lit with diamond hard stars.
Tree sentinels stand, guarding a realm
Drained of all life giving powers.

These are the times of the dead,
For now I sojourn with the shades,
This is my wasteland and all hope has fled,
Leaving shadows in life's masquerade.

Villanellette

Sun low
Red Leaves
Scraggy crow.

Shadows grow
Hearts grieve
Summers go.

Gales blow
Meadows reived
Slow the plough.

Mist flow
Towards eve
Gathered now.

Hedgerow
Crimson bleeds:
Death's tableau.

Which tomorrow
Will fate weave?
I dunno
Heigh-ho.

We are the Shades

Fading,
In the gloom of perpetual night:
We are the Shades!
Mere husks, old dried up shells,
Whose time is gone
Our influence is no more.
Our summer long is passed,
We are its sere and crackling remnants
Blown down autumn paths,
We are the Shades!

Once measured by our work
That strangest drug.
That worth definer,
Template of our lives
Amid whose engines, yearning's ghost still thrives,
And longs for when
In perfect tune each muscle fibril sang,
In arrogance.
When joyed the un-cynic mind;
But sparkling springs run dry,
Each unique trickle lost
Mid trillions swept, unmarked, into the past
On life's amorphous tides.
Too late we learn the truth:
That vanity of youth time sets aside,
No consolation that
We soon must die,
We are the Shades!

Our voice: unheard!
By those who stampede headlong from their dawn
To where?
Why ask?
The moment grasped and fully lived is all.
Oh! 'Brave New Worlders'
Hasten — Try — Explore!
Join life's fleeting, shallow, bacchanal.
Why listen to: 'the dead'?
They have had their day;
Now is your turn
And you must drown,
In beings deeps.
The sensate pool awaits!
Immediacy fills all your needs for now.
Though endless seem your days.
You must wither too!
This we well know,
We are the shades!

Inconsequential now we wait
Discarded! Obsolescent!
Last year's line!
Senescence claims us, aging essence fills
Dusty bottles, drained vintage wine.
Ancestral voices taunt, for you as we
Must bear indignities bequeathed by age,
As time creeps on you'll find new doubts and fears
Until you meet that moment set for all
To pass beyond pass unknowing's waiting door.
There what unimagined demons lurk?
Thus hope!
That peace may fall with death's soft beating wings
Till then we'll wait,
We are the Shades!

Derelicts of shadow and of tomb,
Guilty of unpardonable sin!
Condemned to wander Erebus —
Our crime?
We broke youths golden rule
Becoming old!

Thus here I mourn
For lost, lush-languid lips,
That beauty of those dark and dangerous eyes,
Soft summer skies
Under which I drank such wanton wine;
And squandered ten lives passions
In those nights.
Yet reckless of the cost
I called for more.

Love locked we often lay
Until first light;
Exhausted,
Drunken with the surfeit of desire.

Loves passing is the hardest thing to bear.
Oh precious yesterday!

Presumed unending times,
Where did those sweet dreams go?
Which tiptoed off
While I dozed unaware.

Now all are gone
Vanished with that immemorial throng
Of those who learned
In that instant,
Just before they ceased to be,
It matters not how ravishing the dawn,
Its glory fades
To leave a dying echo in dusk's glades
For those who long for light
Where night pervades.
We are the shades!

The Gates

The gates of Hell crank open through November,
Time's frozen hand hangs cobwebs round the moon;
Life dims, enfeebled, now a dying ember,
In black-basaltic halls of winter gloom.

Oh where was love and why? I can't remember.
The pointlessness of being shrouds my room.
As day by day I trudge through bleak December
Till snowdrop signs of spring will lift my gloom.

Lawyer Autumn

The virgin: May, has lost her fresh green gown,
And matron: August, all her rich attire;
Now lawyer: Autumn, dons his robe of brown
As all the world for death seems to suspire.
He scatters Winter's writs as parchment leaves,
And then with affidavits penned in gloom
Swears all must wither through this sad disease
Which takes a year, which none may then exhume.
Yet in his doleful chambers burns a rose
Defiant scarlet beauty, promising
Time's passing must this subfusc earl depose
Restoring to her throne the princess: Spring.
    Which tort does beauty breach which ends the light,
    Till challenged by the appellant snowdrop, white.

Drowning

Time is running out!
It always was, it always is.
I search for certainty,
But always I find doubt,
Amid the dull fantastical parade of days
In which I live.

Slow slides the moon in beauty
Phase by phase,
And endless aching seasons come and go.
Some clear tomorrow
May yet cure my souls malaise,
Before I drown in death's vast undertow

But time is running out is running out.

Old Shadows

Now night again is longer than the day
And years are few, I wonder what remains?
And though what light there is falls: weeping-grey,
Beauteous breezes warm these darkling lanes
As if the seasons somehow had gone wrong.
This strangeness with imagination plays,
Disturbing as I wander, lone, among
The ruins of this month of dark malaise.
I feel slow ancient rhythms move to where
Old shadows fill forever, and I know
That time the reaper comes and will declare
That all of restless life is ending now.
  The dream of our fulfilment ends in death
  Here promised by sad autumn's dying breath.

Emptying the Bin

I trundle the bin down the drive
—*Another week gone.*
Each weary step squelches rotting leaves underfoot
—*Autumn's refuse.*
The barrenness of the season hangs in the air
—*Almost palpable.*
This Tuesday morning rite, measuring, in imperceptible gradations
—*The route to my demise.*
Trees writhe in a chaotic black emptiness
—*Like weirds in a Boch triptych.*
The frustrations and the small delights of the previous week, here
—*Laid to rest in a plastic bag.*
A sliver of seven days, excised from my life
—*By time's inexorable scalpel.*
With nights haemorrhaging from my diminishing supply
—*Perhaps I should be gasping like a dying man.*
Rather than calmly clinging to these small rituals
—*Which mark out our existence, in small parcels.*

—*Oh g'morning Mr Bell, nice day!*
I leave the bin and quickly turn retracing my steps;
—*What was I thinking?*

The sun emerges from the cloud
—*In an instant my world turns rose and gold.*
Ah! The delightful fickleness of mood.

The season of Despair

In this cavern of air hangs the last evening light,
Reluctant to vanish once more.

From the edge of the world now the cloud dragon wings,
To shade autumn's bright-death coloured floor.

Still a searing blue sash with its yellowing edge,
Mourns for meadow soft summer perfume.

Now through Halloween's door comes the season I dread,
That of darkness and demons of gloom.

In the shadowless night now the Grey Lady glides,
Down the path between crossroads and hall.

For a memory remains of the old family, gone;
Where sad graves hold their bones near the wall.

The six rood lane's threat and the Calvary's might
Mark her bounds and must silence her sighs.

Did a gibbet's cage fright all who looked on that sight?
As old crows made dead holes of her eyes?

Are these figments of dread; phantasms of mind?
Which come as the long night entombs.

Now I live with the shades in my underworld tomb
Till spring's coming, my spirit exhumes.

The Tree

Its branches rose like the arms of a supplicant;
High,
Resisting gravity,
Worshiping some unknown god;
Appealing to the heavens
In graceful obsequies,
Swaying in the wind.
It stood in my way!

I took that old tool, man tool, war tool
— Axe!
And swung its tempered razored-wedge-head high,
Hafting the shaft, two handed, satisfied;
And brought its dead-star-core-mass down —
With violent intent
And the wood was wounded,
White scarred, bitten deep!
Strong sinews groaned, the mighty tree's, and mine.
Mine singing with the work
And its, in vain resistance
In half imagined pain.
Blade rose and fell,
An ugly vee grew wider with each stroke
Until trunk creaked and groaned and swayed,
And fell out of the air to meet the ground.

Two years had passed
And from the stump a leafy fan had grown
Like some wild crown.
Life exerts a strange tenacious will
To live! Survive!
Its purpose to fulfil?

I left it there: reborn,
I grows strong still.

Through Beauty Now

Through beauty now my season wends,
Down sacred paths which lead to light:
To find that dream which never ends.

In lazy days my year extends
Past mists laid low on fields contrite;
Through beauty now my year extends.

Gold-yellow-scarlet leaf-weave lends
A vision leading, through delight,
To find that dream which never ends.

November's velvet sky defends
Stark crystal splendour of the night;
Through beauty now my season wends.

At eventide rich stillness sends:
Contentment, when the mind takes flight
To find that dream, which never ends.

My autumn villanelle contends,
Now we are past Walpurgis Night:
Through beauty now this season wends
To find that dream which never ends.

Vanished Youth

Oh! vanished youth, remember well
That promise of some winsome dream.
The year soon tolls its final knell!

A story strange some poets tell,
Of loves vast, lost, demesne;
Oh! Vanished youth, remember well.

A time in heaven and in hell!
What did those wild nights mean?
The year soon tolls its final knell!

Where are those days which rushed pell-mell?
As though they'd never been,
Oh! Vanished youth, remember well.

Now falling leaves, low mists, foretell
Of endings it would seem;
The year soon tolls its final knell!

Thus ends my autumn villanelle;
Tonight is Halloween!
Oh! Vanished youth, remember well
The year soon tolls its final knell!

A hardly noticed year

A hardly noticed year sinks in decline;
That's nothing special, years just come and go,
All vanish — swallowed by charybdic time,
Chapters snatched from some vast shadow show.
In fragments from that artifice called life,
That maze, through which we wander, mostly lost!
In love, confused, not knowing left from right,
We sometimes find an exit, at what cost?
Important moments pass — peripheralised,
While trivial troubles, worthless hours attract
Until our little span is finalised,
None have not fulfilled that last contract.
     Why ponder on the grief which years endow?
     Enjoy your pagan autumn's beauty now!

These are the months

These are those months when strange and restless moods
Provoke dark thoughts as night replaces day,
When warm transmutes to cold in barren woods,
Where burning leaves must moulder and decay.
Here berries — Satan-black or poison-bright
Are hung as though to make some witches brew,
And spells are cast which turn day to midnight
In which death's shadows all my hopes subdue.
For all my dreams which first took shape in spring,
Then through long summer turned to gold like grain,
Which mellow autumn saw to harvesting;
Are vanished now and may not come again.
    These are the months of strange and restless moods
    When fractured dreams with errant death colludes.

Nights of Rare and Dark Delight

Short days limp slowly: lonely spavined dregs,
Which through November march to close the year.
Sharp bites a north-sent wind whose shrill moan begs
Last leaves to fall, in woods grown dark and drear.
Grassy tussocks in pale mounds look dead
Where once a meadow-sea swelled, waving green;
Sky-swooping-graceful-swallows, all, are fled;
Just lone, home plodding crows, at dusk are seen.
Yet now come nights of rare and dark delight
When star-crowd constellations, locked in time,
Bring those hours when earth bound dreams take flight
Into vast realms carved out in light sublime.
    Late autumn days mark out mortality
    Its nights though reach back through eternity.

I Leave the Grange

I leave the Grange to run the afternoon
Through fields and autumn smells, blown from the sea.
Here wild winds and the swelling clouds commune
Above those white whipped waves, now cresting free.
I burst down to the bar across old stones
And pound the beach above the foaming tide,
Amid storm battered groynes old green streaked bones,
Round pools where secret crabs and bivalves hide.
Within that moment flares the sun, that sight:
Ethereal — a Turnerscape unfolds —
A yacht rides light in riot, grey and white,
That vivid scene my mind forever holds.
    Why come these gifts when random parts collude,
    I ponder as I run, in solitude.

Leaves do not Rustle

Leaves do not rustle they mournfully hiss:
Last breaths through the parched lips of autumn.
Their sibilant sighs seem to murmur a mass
For the days of their youth in the bright sun.
Their colours of dying run bright in the vein;
Russet, burnt sorrel, vermillion, all rain
Down as wild gusts pluck that withered array,
At crepe shrouded dusk whirled forever away,
For the forest must rest wrapped in mouldering decay
As the night shadows stretch ever longer;
And tomb-solemn black now reproaches short day
As the deathly dark wood resumes slumber.
    Listen, now, as November's gales bustle,
    You will hear that the leaves do not rustle.

Rain Swept November

Dark brown, dry-frizzled, a few yet remain
Scattered hawthorn leaves on the high branches.
With a trunk glistening black in the slattering rain
Which, wind slanted, beats fierce then drenches.
The Ivy broods, dark, knowing autumn has come,
Its lowly green marking slow days as they wane,
With its cousin the holly it drinks the brief sun:
Alone in the wood through the winter they'll reign.
Now sodden paths squelch, heaped with leaf mould,
Sky-lined-trees stand starkly as day and night merge;
Summer's wild grandeur lies cast away: old;
Now a distant wind whistles its funeral dirge.
    Light turns to darkness, all beauty decays;
    Rain swept November you sombre my days.

What was that!

What was that!
Sleeking across the ploughed October field
In the half gale
Was it hare or hound?

I take a second look,
No! Just a plastic supermarket bag,
One of those mindless emblems of our age,
A sterile reminder of our soulless times
Gambolling and darting as if alive;
Swirling nowhere with the fallen leaves:
Those immemorial symbols of decay,
"Yellow and black and pale and hectic red!"

This modern interloper on the scene
Jar my sensibilities somehow,
Defiling Shelley's dream.

Youth's Lovely Prime

Youth's lovely prime is stolen from the year
And summer's glories now are memories,
October's gold has tumbled down time's weir;
All lives and loves have met their destinies.
Why should splendour fade with aching time?
Why should beauty wither and decay?
Why should age replace those days sublime,
Which in spring before us, endless, lay?
Yet we have lived and should feel no regret
That soon we pass beyond death's mystery;
Perhaps other realms of beauty wait us yet
Beyond that great unknown and boundless sea.
    Great Autumn's currents hurry me along,
    To where? I leave behind this dreamer's song.

Wotan's Ravens

With bleak far seeing eyes, on deadly wing,
They trudge through empty time
Above men's warring tribes;
The Volsung's heirs, and others, they observe.

Some twenty wars at present, dead disgorge;
The ravens pick their eyes.
No heroes these, unfit for Valkyric hands:
Ignoble charnel heaped by death's machine.

The whole of Africa it seems, in conflict writhes;
With discontent the world of Islam seethes,
As chaos claims the lands which eastward lie
The glutton: West, for now, enjoys its feast.

Grim portents mount, we reap the whirlwind soon;
Such carnage will this next millennium bring!
Thus back to Wotan now you ravens fly
Seek lost Valhalla with your eerie call.

Past Bifrost's rim seek out the funeral pyre
In long lost ashes seek out Loge's fire
His feeble spark will lead to Asgard's door.
The runes run well, inform your noble lord;
Man's end is near: the gods may soon return.

Vespertine

Autumnal flavours flow
In richly flavoured years,
Life-death surrounds me now;
Brief breath, why waste on prayers.

I am of winter's iron,
Heart colder than death's fears,
A brooding cynic's scion;
How pointless fall life's tears.

Youth's raging flood must slow;
Its rhymes heaped round our biers,
All that we are or know
Turn dust down long lost years.

Eve's tolling vesper bell
Warns that the darkness nears
Comes silence or comes hell,
Who knows what dream appears?

Enjoy that which you know
For autumn's beauty cheers
Unique in life's rich flow
Cascading down time's weirs.

The Wren

A bare seen flicker dives towards my room,
The windowpane unseen, the Wren is down!
I race to gather up the bird, concerned
This fragile form may joyous flight resume;
Its purpose: gracing day with fleeting brown
In swift drawn beauty, almost undiscerned.

Its eyes grow glazed; I feel the awful wrench
Of death and inward groan: what purpose is fulfilled?
Now lying in my hand a small life, finished
All that's left is pity and that abject sense:
Of chaos and no god. I am diminished.

Credo

I had a strange dream of hidden ways
Where the grass was several green,
Where the air was still and light hung grey
And we had never been!

Where the life that was is the life that is,
Unchanging, in no pain.
Where the hard gods came then paled and left
For — pointless they remain.

Equilibrium ruled; what flowed returned
And mountains never wore,
And eternal waves from eternal seas
Beat a pre-eternal shore.

But I awoke to the world of change
Of chaos and decay,
Where rules the god of entropy
And death must have his way.

Yet — let me exist in the freezing mist
Near the falling falcon's roar
Where the ice-wind screams through the savage ghyll
To the time scarred savage Tor.

Let me dive deep where the rip tides heap
And the sudden surf descends.
In old age's thrall let me hear youth call
To where life lust never ends.

Let my being flare as a meteor — bare,
In the silken black night air;
Then — in extremis end, knowing I descend
Without fear or hope or care.

If I was asked if I would choose—
In unchanging peace to dwell,
I must reply: let loose life's rage,
Let me test the gates of Hell!

Ironies

What ironies those passing seasons leave
Which mount forever in our dim-lit days,
In which we find delight or learn to grieve,
While wandering through time's uneasy ways.
Unprepossessing chaos here could rule?
Or some immortal's dictat may hold sway?
The one who knows for certain: that poor fool
Must on his altar cast all hope away.
Yet, autumn's idylls resonate once more
And deep from ancient reservoirs still flow
Those inklings which no human should ignore:
That somehow life is held in veiled escrow!
    Does autumn's beauty promise what might come
    Or merely taunt that soon your hour is done!

Of Late I Sense Bright Seraphims

Of late I sense bright Seraphims
around me in the night.
They give my wounded psyche peace,
and ease my doubter's plight.
I have not found religion though,
Its edifices pain.
Its snares and dogmas tell me that
those gods could never reign.
I sense the trans-dimensional,
which guides me to the light.
Of late I sense bright Seraphims
around me in the night.

Dreams Harvested

Sol's low angle marks dissolving time
Which sucks away our lives like drying leaves.
Those weary rays foretell that death sublime
Must gather all; to stand like autumn sheaves
In that last field beyond eternity,
Where all our dreams are harvested and done
And our small space in this immensity
Must vanish, with all joys and sorrows won.
And meaning gleaned from shadows and from shards
From glimpses of a purpose still unknown
Must lie in silence, hymned by angel bards
While we drift with lost memories, alone.
    My body must decay and cease to be!
    My spirit though, craves immortality.

In Celebration

The equinox, which ushers autumn in,
Is herald to a season, rich, sublime;
When ripeness fills my woods and leaves begin
To don the darling colours of decline.
Then comes all-hallow's eve, when trees bereft
Of all their beauty stand in mourning groves,
And wistful breezes sigh for they have left
Skies of gold for those of weeping mauves.
Yet now in celebration, time fulfilled,
Droop luscious berries round the streamlets banks
And fruitfulness by nature's bounty willed
Lies stored against dark winter days, with thanks
    From creatures who through winter's fast will win
    Life's gift, until spring's days of hope begin.

These Are the Days

These are the days of mellow aching sun,
When restful rays last-kiss old dying leaves;
Though from these barren fields was harvest won,
Such empty hours have come that my heart grieves.
Grieves for that golden summer, lost in time;
Grieves for youth's lost and seeming endless days;
For perfect ways and matchless skies sublime,
When wheat ears shimmered in late August's haze.
This is the month of sombre last goodbyes
When endings come and we must journey on
When we will find our rest or perhaps what lies,
In fabled realms when our poor journey's done.
    The year is done, the aching sun declines,
    I must depart, bequeathing you these lines.

Before It Is Too Late

Before it is too late I urge you: go!
And sit beneath the trees and welcome dawn,
And watch the exhumed mists assemble, slow,
And hear that last most beautiful forlorn
Murmuring of autumn's final days.
For soon the months of gloom and cold descend,
For light must abdicate these golden ways
Then shadows fall, which seem can never end.
But now enjoy the last of that most rare:
Perfection, as bright day puts paid to night;
Remembering, if ever comes despair
This time of such sweet beauty and delight.
    The splendour of this season's nearly gone
    But others, in times gift, will soon be won.

Lightning Source UK Ltd.
Milton Keynes UK
13 January 2010
148553UK00002B/1/P

9 780956 083821